moon wisdom

moon wisdom

LUNAR MAGIC AND NATURAL MYSTERIES: A PRACTICAL GUIDE

sally morningstar

southwater

Southwater is an imprint of
Anness Publishing Limited
Hermes House
88-89 Blackfriars Road
London
SE1 8HA
tel. 020 7401 2077
fax 020 7633 9499

Distributed in the UK by
The Manning Partnership
251-253 London Road East
Batheaston
Bath
BA1 7RL
tel. 01225 852 727
fax 01225 852 852

Published in the USA by
Anness Publishing Inc.
27 West 20th Street
Suite 504
New York
NY 10011
tel. 212 807 6739
fax 212 807 6813

Distributed in Australia by
Sandstone Publishing
Unit 1
360 Norton Street
Leichhardt
New South Wales 2040
tel. 02 9560 7888
fax 02 9560 7488

This edition is published by Southwater

10 9 8 7 6 5 4 3 2 1

PUBLISHER: Joanna Lorenz
SENIOR EDITOR: Joanne Rippin
PHOTOGRAPHER: Don Last
STYLING: Lucy Pettifer

ACKNOWLEDGEMENTS
*This book is dedicated with deepest love
to my mother, without whom none of this
would be possible. A special mention for
Joanne Rippin, my editor - she knows
why! I would also like to thank Sue Smith
(astrologer) for her loan of astrological
reference books. Caz, Carmen, Rachel,
Tracy and Kate for being such strong and
faithful female friends, Esther for being a
"woman of a future moon", sister Judy
and all those who have crossed my path
and influenced, shaped and moulded my
own female wisdom in many different
ways.*

Contents

Introduction	6
Moon Facts	8
Moon Myths and Legends	10
Moon Goddesses	12
The Angel of the Moon	14
Animal Totems of the Moon	16
Moon Signs	20
The Lunar Wheel of the Year	32
The Moon's Phases	34
The Moon and Women	38
The Moon and the Weather	40
The Blue Moon	41
Lunar Gardening	42
A Water Garden Feature	45
Lunar Plants	46
The Moon and Numerology	47
Lunar Colours	48
The Moon and the Tarot	50
A Lunar Talisman	52
Moon Crystals	54
Casting a Brightmoon Circle	57
Moon Medicines	58
Psychic Dreams	60
The Sacred Moon Tree	62
Index and Acknowledgements	64

Introduction

THE MOON IS MYSTERIOUS. She is known by many names and is worshipped by many cultures throughout the world, both ancient and modern. Our great Mother Moon inspires wonder when we see her fullness in the sky, shining her silver light upon the shadows of the night. Both men and women are intimately linked to her changing faces of crescent, full, waning and dark, as she progresses through her lunar cycle. When she pulls and tugs at the waters of the earth, creating high and low tides, she also pulls at the water within our bodies, affecting our moods, sleep patterns, health, and women's "moontime" cycles. It is well documented that the full moon has powerful effects upon mental and emotional stability.

Because Mother Moon is well within the gravitational field of the earth, her interaction with us and her elliptical orbit affects weather patterns around the world. Rainfall, tropical

storms, hurricanes and earthquakes have all been associated with lunar influence and activity. She is intimately linked to our world and we are deeply affected by her, as is the planet we inhabit.

This book will take you on a journey to meet Mother Moon, to get to know her and to understand the nature of her rhythms and cycles. Along the way, you can learn how to plant a lunar garden, make a lunar talisman, learn about moon medicines, and discover some of her magical mysteries. The moon is the personification of female wisdom, the wisdom of intuitive knowledge and deep instincts. She cannot be tamed by rational thought: she is a free spirit. May your spirit meet with hers in the pages of this book, and may the secrets of the moon be revealed to you.

CENTRE AND RIGHT: *Because of the interaction of moon and earth, the moon is linked to fertility and childbirth. There are more births at the full moon than at any other time in the lunar cycle, and for thousands of years moon deities, such as the goddess Diana, have been called upon to increase fertility and aid conception.*

Moon Facts

T HE MOON IS THOUGHT to be about 4,600 million years old, the same age as the earth. She measures 3,476 km/2,170 miles across and her gravity – one-sixth that of the earth – exerts an influence upon earth's tidal flows and weather patterns. The earth's electromagnetic field, crop yields and weather are all affected by the moon's cycles.

The Moon's Surface

In 1610, Galileo framed the moon in his telescope for the first time and discovered the details of its rocky and craggy surface. The craters on the moon measure up to 240 km/150 miles across. Some astronomers believe that these are probably the result of impacts from comets and asteroids over millions of years, while others believe that they stem from volcanic activity within the moon itself. The most recent crater, which appears in the south-west quadrant of the moon, is called the Tycho impact basin. These crags and imperfections have led people from past civilizations to see the image of a man in the moon, and to speculate about a lunar population. However, even before we first put a man on the

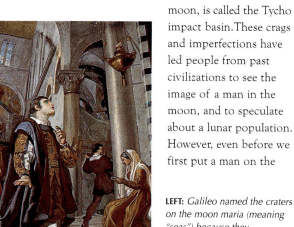

LEFT: *Galileo named the craters on the moon maria (meaning "seas") because they resembled calm oceans, although they are more likely to have been created by volcanic lava than by water.*

LEFT AND OPPOSITE: *Some believe that the moon and the earth were once a single planet, others that the moon was drawn into the earth's force field at some point. Yet another hypothesis is that the two planets were formed together out of the same space dust and cosmic gases. The actual origin of the moon remains a mystery.*

moon, in 1969, it had been established that, with hardly any atmosphere and no water, it was not possible for the moon to sustain life as we know it.

The Lunar Cycle

Because of the moon's elliptical orbit, she can be anything between 356,398 km/222,749 miles and 406,698 km/ 254,186 miles away from earth. This orbit pattern also means that we only ever get to see one side of her. Surface temperatures range from -233°C/-387°F at night to 127°C/ 260°F at midday, as the light of the sun is reflected back from the moon's surface to earth. A moon–sun conjunction creates the image of the crescent, or new, moon, and a full moon occurs when they are in alignment with each other. The moon is slowly pulling away from the earth's gravitational influence, by 3 cm/1¼ in annually, so the length of our daily cycle is increasing by a minuscule amount each year.

It takes the moon 27.3 days to circle the earth, but because earth and moon are spinning together at different speeds around the sun, it actually takes the moon 29 days, 12 hours, 44 minutes and 28 seconds to complete one orbit of the earth, from new moon to new moon.

Moon Myths and Legends

T HE MOON HAS BEEN DEPICTED in ancient texts and legends as both the giver and the taker of life. Because of her ever-changing and yet regenerative cycle, she was seen as immortal and as the place to which souls departed at death. She could bring gentle rains to water the fields but she could also raise storms and ruin crops, so she was considered unpredictable and potentially destructive. Goddesses chosen to represent her were double-sided as well, endowed with both destructive and creative powers.

In many ancient cultures, legends surrounding the dawn of creation concern the sun and moon. In Aztec mythology, the moon was named Xochiquetzal, companion to the sun and protector of lovers. She was also linked to the family, and to childbirth. The Mayans' moon deity was called Ixchel, and

was feared as the bringer of floods and storms. Her skirt was decorated with bones, and her crown was a serpent. Despite this she was also a protector of women in childbirth.

In Sumerian mythology, the principal moon deity was male. Sin, also known as Nanna, was worshipped in the ancient city of Ur (Lemuria). He was associated with the new moon and, like the goddesses of the moon that were worshipped by other cultures, he was responsible for the fertility of the land, for food production and the protection of herds, especially cattle. The re-enactment of the sacred marriage between the male (waxing) and female (waning) aspects of the lunar cycle was undertaken between the king of Ur, embodying the god Sin, and the goddess in the person of a priestess. By performing this ceremony, they were enacting the continuance and co-operation of the two opposites.

In the mythology of many of the North American native tribes, the spider was the weaver of the web of creation, producing the physical world, and then

LEFT: *This limestone relief depicts Sin, the Sumerian moon god, crowned with a crescent moon.*

ABOVE: *Moon festivals of ancient times were often celebrated with music and dance. Music has long been associated with the moon. The sacred dances would climax in orgiastic rites or sacrifices, to ensure good crop yields, fair weather and health for the tribal community.*

supporting and nurturing life on earth. The spider is universally linked to the life-giving qualities of the moon.

The snail, because of its moisture trail and its seeming ability to vanish and reappear, is also linked to the moon. It was thought that the snail could travel into the underworld and re-emerge unharmed. The Mexican moon god, Tecciztecatl, was depicted in the shell of a snail.

Mirrors figure prominently in moon lore, because of their reflective qualities, and have long been used for divination purposes. In Britain, in the 19th century it was a common folk custom for girls to use a mirror and the full moon to see how long it would be before they were married. Two and a half thousand years earlier, it is said that Pythagoras was taught mirror divination by the wise women of Thessaly.

LEFT: *The unicorn represents the lunar power in mythology as the lion does the sun. In heraldry, the two pictured together draw upon the complementary powers of the sun and the moon.*

Moon Goddesses

MANY ANCIENT CIVILIZATIONS venerated the moon because they saw how she influenced the germination and growth of crops, how she matched the average female menstrual cycle of 28–30 days, and how she affected weather, as well as her self-regenerative ability in waxing and waning – appearing and then disappearing again. Even the dark time of the moon was seen to hold secrets about death and the veil that separates spirit from matter. Her ancient worshippers knew her as the "Queen of Heaven", and could see that she held the key to a deep and profound wisdom about the rhythms and cycles of human existence and the natural world.

In order to find ways to express their beliefs, at a time when the structure of the cosmos was still a mystery, they turned to archetypes that personified these beliefs in the form of gods and goddesses. Because it was important to differentiate between the phases of the moon, different goddesses represented each

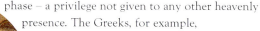

ABOVE: A triform statue of Hecate

RIGHT: The moon goddess Selene pictured here with Endymion by Poussin

ABOVE:
The moon goddess, Venus

phase – a privilege not given to any other heavenly presence. The Greeks, for example, worshipped Artemis as the new moon, Selene as the full moon and Hecate as the waning and dark moon. All the goddesses from across the ages are really one and the same, blending and moving together to weave the powers of the moon into immortal form. Goddesses of the moon were absorbed into other cultures as civilizations evolved. The Greek Artemis became Diana in Rome, for example, and Ma'at, goddess of truth and the consort of the Egyptian moon god Thoth, was known by the Gnostics as Sophia. The cult of the Egyptian goddess Isis, the "Good Mother", spread through Greece and the Roman Empire

ABOVE: *Diana was a Roman triple goddess – the virgin, the mother of nature, and the huntress. As huntress she is the destroyer aspect of the moon.*

Goddesses of the Moon

The moon goddess is also called the "Triple Goddess" because of her three phases, new, full and waning/dark. The Triple Goddess represents the maiden, the mother and the crone and is also known as the "Great Mother" or "Magna Dei". There are also gods of the moon, one is Thoth, the Egyptian god of the moon, another is Sin, the Sumerian god.

Artemis, Greek, carrying a quiver filled with arrows and a bow, accompanied by lionesses, deer and birds: childbirth.

Selene, Greek, wearing wings and a head band, riding in a chariot drawn by white horses: magic.

Diana, Roman, carrying a bow and arrow, with a hound and stag: fertility and nature.

Hecate, Greek, a goddess who has three heads, usually standing back-to-back with horse, hound and lioness: magic, sorcery, death and the underworld.

Sophia of Phrygia, female representation of the holy spirit: divine knowledge and wisdom.

Arianrhod, Celtic, wearing silver robes and holding a silver wheel: divination.

Ceridwen, Celtic dark moon goddess, with cauldron, and white sow: herbs and grains, divination, spells, death.

Isis, (above) Egyptian, wearing a crescent head-dress supporting a full moon: magic, fertility, regeneration.

Cybele, Phrygian, the dark moon goddess, wearing a crescent moon headress, with pomegranates and bees, carrying finger bones: nature, wild beasts and dark magic.

and lasted well into the Christian era, to be absorbed by the cult of the Virgin Mary, who was also a lady of the moon. So strong was the compulsion to honour the moon goddess and keep her favour, that sacrifices and rites were performed in the hope that by appeasing her, she would be sympathetic to human needs for food, water and regeneration. All phases of the moon held secrets about the circle of life. By worshipping the appropriate moon goddess, humans could relate to (and try to tame) her influence.

The Angel of the Moon

A S THE GREAT MOTHER, the moon has considerable influence over her human "children" as do angels. The angel associated with the moon is Gabriel, the healer. Gabriel is usually referred to as "he", although in fact angels are neither male nor female. He is the Angel of the Annunciation, who visited the Virgin Mary (who is a lady of the moon), and his visit is described in a hymn: "The Angel Gabriel from Heaven came, his wings as drifted snow, his eyes as flame". He is sometimes depicted carrying white lilies, the flowers of the Virgin, and is intimately linked with healing and with alleviating suffering on earth.

On the lunar wheel Gabriel stands in the west, in the position of the waning moon. The direction of west is represented by the water element. If you are seeking healing, or performing healing ceremonies for others, stand facing the west during the time of a waning moon (especially if it is in a water sign) to say prayers for healing. You should also face west to make a water offering. A water offering can be anything that is taken from the waters of the earth, such as watercress, a river stone, seaweed or a shell. You may like to seek out a scallop or other large shell and fill it with spring water for any healing ceremonies that you are performing.

ABOVE: *Gabriel is often depicted carrying white lilies, the flower of the Virgin Mary.*

RIGHT: *The power of Gabriel's spiritual flames can charge any environment that he enters. He has dominion over all diseases and so has great healing powers.*

An Angel Healing

Perform this ceremony just after a full moon to seek healing for someone who is sick. Choose camphor, eucalyptus or sandalwood as your fragrant aroma. All these fragrances are linked to the healing qualities of the moon.

You will need
- 2 light blue candles
- crystal
- white lilies
- water offering
- aromatherapy burner
- matches

- 9 drops of eucalyptus, sandalwood or camphor oil
- 9 white nightlights
- pen with silver ink
- natural paper
- heatproof container

1 Put the two blue candles in the centre of a table with the crystal, flowers, water offering and burner. Light the candles and burner. Fill the burner with water and add the oil.

2 Place the nightlights in a circle around the other items and light them all.

3 Write the name of the person requiring healing, and their ailment, on a piece of paper. Fold it up twice and hold it in your hands, saying, "Angel Gabriel I ask for your help. Please bring your healing touch to [name]. By divine will, remove [this condition] from [name], for the highest good of all."

4 Take the piece of paper, light it in the flame of one of the candles then drop it into the heatproof bowl, while visualizing the ailment being lifted out of the person and carried away by Gabriel. Give thanks for the healing vibrations, blow out all the candles and close the healing by putting the nightlights away.

Animal Totems of the Moon

CERTAIN ANIMALS HAVE long and deep links with the moon and have become her totems. In addition to these, any animal linked to moisture, seas, rivers, and lakes, such as the frog, toad or fish, will be pertinent to the moon to some degree.

Wolf

The wolf has been linked with the psychic aspects of lunar lore and with baying at the full moon. Legends about people turning into werewolves at a full moon may be based upon a certain amount of fact. The symptoms of a rare medical condition called lycanthropy, where a patient has fantasies of being a wolf, seem to be triggered by the full moon, and this could be the basis of werewolf legends.

LEFT: *The wolf is strongly linked with psychic aspects of the moon.*

Hare

Pictorial images of the hare have been found in Assyrian reliefs and in ancient Egypt. The myth of the "hare in the moon" is well known in the Far East, Africa, South America and Europe.

The hare represents the lunar cycles: from new to full and waning to dark; from conception to gestation; from growth to decline and death. Long associated with fertility and the fertility cycle, the hare was considered to be androgynous (having both male and female attributes) by ancient cultures. This was representative of the way they perceived the moon: the waxing moon was the male aspect and the waning moon the female aspect.

The Anglo-Saxon goddess of fertility, Eostre, was depicted with the head of a hare, and in many other cultures – including Celtic, Indian, Buddhist, Chinese, and Native American – deities of the moon were illustrated carrying a hare. The Native American hero Manabazho, portrayed as a hare, is an important symbol of creation.

Seek hare medicine when performing fertility rites, prayers, or wishes, when seeking joy and illumination or when needing quick results.

ABOVE: *The spring festival of Eostre, a fertility rite, was the origin of the Christian festival of Easter. The hare is linked to this time of year and is a symbol of the birth of new life and the beginning of a fertile cycle.*

The frog is the bringer of the rains as well as a fertility symbol associated with the moon. Hekt, the frog goddess of the ancient Egyptians, carried the potential of the fertile waters that symbolize birth and fertility, and the green frog found in the Nile region was venerated as the bringer of new life and fruitfulness.

The frog is also a totem clan animal of the Native Americans, for whom it is a symbol of the water element, a powerful cleanser. The sacred Manitou ("Great Spirit") of the Algonquin people lives in the moon and influences the waters of the world, as well as the weather. Weather, like anything associated with water, has a connection with the moon, because of her strong influence upon it.

Seek frog medicine when you are wanting to move from one situation to another without obstacles, when working on cleansing the emotions, and during any fertility prayers.

The cat is an animal that is difficult to get to know, maintaining a certain distance and mystery for us. The cat is associated with the Greek goddess Artemis, known in Roman mythology as Diana. Bast – a cat-headed goddess – was worshipped by the ancient Egyptians; to hurt or destroy a cat in Egypt was punishable by death, because the animals were held in such high esteem.

The cat has long been known as a "familiar" to magical practitioners, especially those who work with lunar magic. In other cultures, too, the mythology of the cat can be seen as important. For example, Shosti, the Hindu goddess of childbirth, is depicted riding one, and Freya, the Norse goddess of love and fertility, is shown riding in a cat-drawn carriage. The cat, as a symbol of the moon, represents her mystery. During the Christian era the black cat has been relegated to the realms of witchcraft and sorcery rather than being seen as a representative of the moon's teachings.

Seek cat medicine when you want to improve your psychic abilities, or during psychic protection ceremonies. Call on the goddess Bast when looking for a lost cat, as she has great influence with feline creatures.

ABOVE: *It was long thought that the souls of the dead were carried by frogs to the moon. Frog talismans, which have been discovered in ancient Egyptian tombs, are likely to have been symbols of resurrection into the spirit world of the moon.*

ABOVE: *Part of human domestic life but also leading an independent life of mystery, particularly at night, the cat's affinity to the moon is profound.*

LEFT: *The cow is also associated with the moon, because her horns look like the crescent or new moon.*

Sacred animal of Isis, the mother goddess of ancient Egypt, the cow represents fertility. She is also the giver of milk that nourishes human life, as well as the life of her calf. Milk, like water, is associated with the gifts of the moon.

The moon goddess was worshipped in ancient Egypt as a golden, long-horned cow. At the winter solstice, Isis, crowned as the moon-cow, would circle the coffin of her consort, Osiris, seven times. This symbolized the seven circlings of the moon from winter to summer, signifying the turning of the wheel to new life and the resurrection of the universal spirit.

People of the buffalo clan in Native American Indian traditions are the prayer weavers; seek bovine medicine or the assistance of the sacred cow, or use items symbolizing the cow when saying prayers, when asking for blessings, and when seeking spiritual illumination.

Owls represent wisdom and are most commonly heard on a night of the full moon during the winter months, remaining silent for most of the rest of the year. Linked to Hecate, goddess of the dark moon, the owl will often be significantly noticed just before the death of someone close. Rather than being of evil intent, the sound of the owl's call, or the sudden or unusual appearance of one, should be seen as reassurance that the spirit of the moon is calling to help the soul back to its true home.

The owl can also represent deep fears, the unconscious, and fear of the dark. Hearing an owl close by may not signify a death, but rather a call to understand something about yourself, that resides deep within your psyche. Seek the wisdom of owl medicine when trying to deepen your connection with the inner teacher, or when you are in a spiritual or life-changing crisis.

ABOVE: *The owl is a harbinger of death and is associated with Hecate, the goddess of the dark moon.*

Other animals associated with the moon are the toad, the lion, the bear and the fox. In Chinese mythology, a three-legged toad represents the yin, or female, aspect of life, and the traditional explanation for a lunar eclipse was that the toad had swallowed the moon. Some Native American tribes associate the toad with the dark phase of the moon's cycle – in other words, the deeper, more silent time where wisdom can be taught and found. The lion has long represented the powers of the sun, but the lioness is said to represent the powers of the moon and several cultures have depicted lionesses with lunar deities.

ABOVE: The lioness is sacred to the Phrygian goddess, Cybele.

The bear is linked to the moon goddess Diana. As one of the great shamanic animals, said to be responsible for teaching the sacred medicine way, it is no surprise that the bear came to be associated with the teachings of the moon's wisdom.

The fox, long known for his cunning and ability to shapeshift, is known in North America and Japan as the bringer of rain. As such, he has links with the atmospheric influences of the moon upon the weather.

Moon totem animals can be carried as charms or talismans, which should ideally be made of silver, the metal of the moon. Dreams about any of the moon totem animals could well signify that an important change is imminent, or may signify a time of increased fertility (such as ovulation), a birth, death of the old, or a time for learning and growth.

Animal Associations with the Triple Goddess

New moon: hare, cow, frog – Artemis, the maiden.

Full moon: bear, dove, hare, cow, cat, frog, wolf, stag – Diana, Isis, Selene, Arianrhod, the mother.

Waning and dark moon: owl, serpent, hound, bat, fox, toad – Hecate, Ceridwen, Cybele, the crone.

LEFT: *Isis wore a headdress that symbolized her virtues and associations. Her crown is a crescent moon supporting the full moon.*

BELOW: *In Celtic mythology, the bear was a lunar power, also associated with King Arthur.*

Moon Signs

IN ASTROLOGY, the position of the sun at birth represents your outer personality, whereas the position of the moon indicates your inner world of feelings and emotions. To discover the position of the moon at your birth, you will need to consult an astrologer for a natal chart. Once this has been established, you can refer to the information in the relevant section below.

Moon in Aries

Aries moon people tend to be impulsive and hasty, with a tendency to make quick (and sometimes rash) decisions. Their impulsiveness can make them impatient, and so increase the probability of accidents because of the speed at which they like to travel. They have quick and agile minds and are natural leaders, but need to guard against being bossy, overbearing, arrogant, or dismissive of others. If they learn how to harness this moon's powers, they can become excellent leaders, public speakers and pioneers.

Aries moons crave independence and can feel very trapped by possessive or jealous behaviour. They do not understand the depths of emotions or feel particularly comfortable with them. As this is a fire moon, their feelings are very self-orientated. In fact, of all the faults that an Aries moon may have, selfishness is the greatest challenge to overcome.

They are forward thinkers, inspired by new and challenging opportunities, wanting to carve their own path through life. People with their moon in Aries will be innovators in business, but need to learn to follow through anything they start. However, because of their "go it alone" attitude, Aries moons can sometimes be insensitive and thoughtless. Once a deeper understanding of this moon is reached, they will often regret things that they have said or done through lack of sensitivity and will then try to make up for it in some way.

ABOVE: *When the moon is transiting Aries, there will be an increase in fiery energy, leading to the potential for confrontations, but by remaining sensitive to others Aries moons can motivate without dominating. Arguments aside, this moontime is excellent for calling in the new and for taking steps towards a goal, bringing as it does an upsurge of willpower and determination.*

Stones:
diamond, bloodstone

Flower:
wild rose

Animal:
ram

Moon in Taurus

People with their moon in Taurus are easy-going, relaxed and generally fun to be with. They appreciate fine art, music and the creative arts as well as good food. Taurus moons are happy hosts, enjoying entertaining and providing entertainment to friends and family alike. These people are sensualists, with a love of beautiful things. They can, however, have a tendency to get stuck in ritual and routine. They dislike change and may be stubborn and inflexible, unless, of course, it is their own decision to change. They will not be pushed into anything.

Taurus moons are careful with money. Being materialistic, they like to buy good-quality products and will work hard to be able to afford them. This moon's message is that life is for enjoying, but they must guard against becoming addicted to rich and unhealthy foods. A healthy diet is vital for the Taurus moon, or their constitution will be weakened.

Taurus moons can feel very threatened by any challenges to their family life, and will do anything to maintain security. They are sensitive to the opinions of neighbours and the community, and are traditionalists. Their conformist attitudes can sometimes be stifling to those around them – possessiveness is the greatest challenge they have to overcome. Above all, Taurus moons are practical and down-to-earth. They provide a safe environment for children to grow up in, but need to allow their children to express their true personalities and not what is acceptable or expected of them. Letting the children go is the hardest lesson for Taurus moon parents.

Stones:
emerald

Flower:
rose

Animal:
bull

ABOVE: *When the moon is passing through Taurus, be careful with your possessions, ensuring your home is secure if you need to go away. Take care of personal finances, and practical matters. When the new moon is in Taurus, it is a good time to begin longer term projects that may take a while to come to fruition.*

Moon in Gemini

ABOVE: *When the moon is transiting Gemini it is an important time to make sure that everything is based on fact, not to get carried away, and to guard against being too flippant about responsibilities. Be aware that stress will be an issue during this time, with an increase in the possibility of nervous tension and exhaustion.*

People with their moon in Gemini are mentally agile, flitting from one idea to another with great ease. With this natural tendency, Gemini moons will have many projects on the go and need to learn to complete what they begin. Loose tongues need to be guarded against – Gemini moons can be gossips and chatterboxes, because of their love of the spoken word (and the sound of their own voices). The greatest challenges for Gemini moons are an appreciation of silence and the consolidation of actions.

Boredom sets in quickly with this placement, because their minds are constantly thinking up better ideas or solutions to problems. Their quick-wittedness and versatility is therefore a strength as well as a potential weakness. Once understanding of how to harness an agile mind into practical action is mastered, this sign is an asset in many situations. However, because of their tendency to move on quickly (unless the conversation is fascinating), they often miss opportunities to learn from, or understand, others.

Gemini moons find emotional people difficult to be around, and often have difficulty expressing their own feelings. They are drawn to the lighter side of life, where chatting and social interaction prevail. As long as they have stimulating outlets for their inspirations and sociability, they will be happy and content. They make excellent speakers, teachers, journalists and anything associated with the use of language.

Gemini parents like to stimulate the minds of their children, providing them with opportunities for exploration. They find it difficult to remain constant but are fun to be with and will spend hours at play with their family.

Stones:
agate

Flower:
lavender

Animal:
monkey

Moon in Cancer

The moon is exalted in Cancer. This means that she is in her best placement here. The moon governs this zodiacal sign and so will be a powerful influence in the chart when placed here. Cancer moon people are highly sensitive and crave emotional security. They need to be accepted for who they are, so can become extremely defensive when challenged. They are sensitive to atmospheres and are very intuitive. Their feelings are often correct, but they need to guard against presuming they are correct all the time, falling into the negative trap of feeling wronged, hurt or rejected. Learning how to accept the feelings and opinions of others will bring a great release to the anxieties that can be experienced by Cancer moons.

Cancer moon people are the carers of the zodiac, taking on the sick and the weak in order to care for those less fortunate than themselves. This does not challenge their position and yet gives them the opportunity to excel in what they do best, but this caring should not be allowed to spill over into obsessional behaviour. They must learn to let others make their own mistakes and try not to rescue everyone they perceive is in need.

They can be possessive and clingy in relationships, often retreating from areas of conflict instead of discussing them. They have a tendency towards self pity and sometimes have a moody and unpredictable side. They will not reveal anything until they are ready. They can also over-exaggerate as their emotions take them on a roller-coaster of different realities and conclusions. They often think and expect the worst.

Cancer moon women can suffer more than most from pre-menstrual tension.

Stones:
moonstone

Flower:
water lily

Animal:
crab

ABOVE: *Cancer moon people make ideal parents because of their desire to be needed, they are sensitive, caring and supportive of their children. When the moon is transiting Cancer, it is a good time to spend with the family, or help others. Try to avoid depressing situations, which will be prevalent during this time.*

Moon in Leo

ABOVE: *At a time when the moon is transiting Leo, electrical equipment can go wrong, so it is not a good time to shop for new gadgets or appliances especially for Leo moon people. Guard against being self-centred, over-opinionated or pushy when in this phase.*

People with their moon in Leo are naturally gregarious and love being the centre of attention. They know little fear and will have a go at most things, believing that everything is attainable. They may tend to be bossy and self-centred, believing, as they do, that they are the best at everything. This is a double-edged tendency, because they can also be great motivators to others who lack their level of confidence. Leo moons love the limelight and may well be attracted to the creative arts, theatre, dance, or anything that allows them self-expression. They need to ensure that they find ways to balance their extrovert side with steadying activities that slow them down a little. They can bombard their way through life, completely unaware of their effect upon others, as they climb to the top.

Above all, Leo moons need to be recognized and appreciated. Like the lioness, Leo moon people are proud and able. They love romance and romantic interludes, and may often have a string of admirers who adore them. It is important to learn humility when your moon is in Leo and to sprinkle this over a naturally flamboyant lifestyle.

Caution is not the strongest characteristic when the moon is placed here. Think before you act, and plan before you begin, otherwise several very creative ideas may get lost in a whirl of self-aggrandizement.

Leo moons are sociable and enjoy mixing with others. As parents, they see their children as extensions of their own egos, and so will push them to succeed. This pressure can be negative and result in driving a child away early from the home, if they find the levels of control or domination are just too overwhelming.

Stones:
ruby

Flower:
sunflower

Animal:
lion

Moon in Virgo

Moon in Virgo people are discriminating and exacting. They are extremely clean and tidy – meticulous, in fact. Everything has its place when the moon is in this sign. Virgo moons are tactful and diplomatic, so make excellent peacemakers and negotiators.

Virgo moon people tend to be nervous and highly strung, lacking a basic confidence in their abilities. Their way with words can sometimes be wonderful, and writers often have their moon in this sign. They need to guard against being too critical or judgmental: their high standards and expectations can make others feel inadequate or uncomfortable. They are highly practical, and excel in most things they attempt, because they are methodical in their approach. Their attention to detail means that their homes are spotless, their offices organized, and all plans are made with care, leaving little room for error. This strictness can be limiting sometimes, and learning a level of flexibility and fluidity can, therefore, be highly beneficial. Virgo moons are generally conscientious about their health, but need to guard against becoming fitness gurus to friends and family, because of their own obsessions with health.

Virgo moons are steady and reliable partners, good at handling and investing money. They approach parenting in the same way as everything else – with orderly correctness. The children are well turned out, their rooms are clean and tidy and everything is "taken care of" on a practical level. However, paranoia about mess can cause friction in the family and Virgo moon parents need to learn to loosen up and allow their children the freedom to get themselves dirty once in a while.

Stones:
jade

Flower:
buttercup

Animal:
cat

ABOVE: *When the moon is transiting Virgo, issues surrounding health and exercise will arise. This is a good time to begin a healthy eating plan or begin regular visits to the gym, as well as having a medical check-up. Keep things practical, and try not to be too critical and judgmental during this moon.*

Moon in Libra

Moon in Libra people love beauty and harmony. They are naturally charming and likeable, able to see many different points of view. This makes them excellent diplomats, lawyers or politicians. This ability, however, can also be a hindrance, leaving Libra moons uncertain and indecisive: decision-making is quite distasteful to them.

They are understanding and sensitive to the thoughts and feelings of others, which means that they can often be used as a shoulder to cry on, or a place of refuge. However, other people would be wise to understand that the Libra moon's sensitivity can also be withdrawn if it is taken for granted or seen as a weakness.

Libra moons love beautiful things and the good things in life. Being naturally creative, their homes are artistically decorated and put together, even if little money is available. This artistic streak can also extend into their working lives with a job in the performing or visual arts, such as theatre, painting, dance or music.

They fall in love easily and enjoy their relationships, having a need to relate to other people. They must, however, avoid escapism and learn to face up to their own faults. Disharmony in the home can lead quite quickly to ill health, producing headaches and physical tension.

Libra parents want to share their cultured interests with their children, involving them in the arts in some form or other. This can lead to conflicts, if the children have no interest in such things. Libra moon parents need to allow their offspring to develop their own identity, follow their own particular talents and allow their creativity to shine however they choose.

ABOVE: Moon in Libra people reside where there is harmony, creating lovely homes with relaxing environments. When the moon is passing through Libra it is a good time to focus upon harmony within relationships, but not a time to make any serious decisions.

Stones:
opal

Flower:
violet

Animal:
hare

Moon in Scorpio

People with their moon in Scorpio will be intensely secretive and difficult to fathom, and any hurts will be stored away for a long, long time. Scorpio moons need to have the company of positive friends to help to lift them out of these depths into the fresh air of fun and laughter. The lighthearted side of life often escapes them, and they are sometimes much too serious, or even moody. This can lead to drug abuse or addictive patterns of behaviour. Scorpio moons need to learn how to channel their feelings into such things as self-healing, team games, and a healthy routine, instead of turning any negativity on to others or, even worse, upon themselves.

Scorpio moons can, however, utilize their intuitive skills in medicine, research, healing and detective work, and they are happiest when left to get on with a task quietly. Talented, because of their deep nature, Scorpio moons may end up in positions of power, but will be bosses that no one really understands. This is because Scorpio moons have difficulty with trust and openness.

In relationships, they have a lot to give, if they will let go enough to give it. They should learn not to bear grudges or carry hurt feelings for too long, learning instead how to forgive and move on.

Scorpio moon parents are fiercely protective of their offspring, sometimes bordering on possessiveness and jealousy, and do not welcome advice. They need to understand that children need a diversity of relationships in order to develop a well-rounded sociability. Any over-protectiveness is extremely supportive when necessary, but stifling when it is not.

Stones:
topaz

Flower:
chrysanthemum

Animal:
eagle

ABOVE: *When the moon is passing through Scorpio, feelings will run deep, and destructive attitudes and explosive arguments are possible. This is not the time to talk about important or sensitive issues, but to get on with some positive activity like decorating or gardening instead.*

ABOVE: *When the moon is passing through Sagittarius, things may not go according to plan, taking different turns to the ones planned for or expected. It is a time to be adaptable and to think of other ways to achieve your goals. Travel plans may well be highlighted or have to be changed.*

Moon in Sagittarius

Sagittarius moon people are gregarious, funny, witty and tactless. Often speaking without thinking, these people need to learn how to be sociable without putting their foot in it. Sagittarius moons are highly independent and individualistic, not worrying too much about what others think of them, since they hold quite a high opinion of their own abilities anyway.

They are very able, but a lack of sensitivity can sometimes mean that they tread on other people as they climb or travel to the top. They are mentally agile, with a love of and a need for freedom, often championing causes and following political concerns for the benefit of other people. They rise to a challenge, but need to guard against carelessness, including carelessness with money. Gambling is a strong temptation when the moon is placed here. Sagittarius moons can be reckless and would benefit from learning to pay attention to detail.

They have a naturally carefree attitude, which sometimes borders upon restlessness if their intellect is not sufficiently stimulated. Their work needs to be stimulating and challenging, so that they can rise to the task. This moon placement can bring great wisdom, if the carefree attitude is tempered with sensibility.

They make good partners and are probably among the best parents in the zodiac. However, if things start to go wrong in a relationship you will not see Sagittarians for dust. They will have left already, looking for a more optimistic landscape in which to champion their causes. Generally happy people, they find it hard to stay where they feel uncomfortable.

Stones:
sapphire

Flower:
carnation

Animal:
horse

Moon in Capricorn

People with their moon in Capricorn will be hard-working, perhaps even workaholics. They have an almost fanatical dedication to making money and becoming successful, often at the expense of personal relationships. If other areas of the astrological chart are well starred, they can become very wealthy and perhaps even famous. However, this placement is not an easy one, and lunar Capricorns often have to make sacrifices, putting their own emotional needs aside for the good of the family, children, or anyone apart from themselves, which can lead them to become martyrs, with a tendency to moan about their lot. Capricorn moons can suffer with allergies and skin complaints, and benefit from being spontaneous, especially at those times when the limitations of martyrdom are affecting their health.

Women with their moon in Capricorn often put their feelings aside and settle with a partner who will provide them with material security – because this is seen as a need with this placement. Capricorn moon men, on the other hand, will often connect with a woman who can further their career – planning everything to their best personal advantage. This is not a sign that is willing to take risks.

Emotions do not figure strongly with Capricorn moons, and there can be a tendency to aloofness and detachment. This is sometimes balanced with a warm and funny sense of humour which rises spontaneously and can help to balance the rather superior, rigid exterior so often presented to the world.

Parents of this moon sign expect their children to work hard and do well and often need to accept their children for who they really are.

Stones:
onyx

Flower:
pansy

Animal:
goat

ABOVE: *When the moon is passing through Capricorn, it is a good time to work on your finances, and attend to any practical matters. Capricorn men and women set great store by financial security and advancement and will put aside emotional matters if necessary.*

Moon in Aquarius

ABOVE: *When the moon is passing through Aquarius, there will be an increase in creative and metaphysical ideas, with the opportunity to perform charitable acts. This phase of the moon is a good time to celebrate life; to have a party, or invite some friends over for inspiring conversations.*

People with the moon in Aquarius can be highly original thinkers and extremely creative, often following a career in the performing or creative arts. They are interesting, unusual and will have many fascinated friends. However, Aquarius moons must guard against careless talk or flippant actions at times when life is too dull or humdrum for them. Although friendly and well-meaning, these people are not always the wisest when it comes to tact and diplomacy. They need to find a balance between innovative ideas and practical actions, and to avoid getting carried away with the next brilliant brainwave before it proves to be workable. They are outspoken and inventive. As lovers of freedom, they are often drawn to improving society in some way. Their need for independence runs deep, and Aquarius moons hate to be tied down.

Aquarius moons have a deep interest in metaphysical issues, the occult and supernatural phenomena. They frequently present mysterious and magnetic qualities that draw the unusual to them. They can be secretive and difficult to fathom because of this rather enigmatic predisposition.

Aquarius moons are unpredictable, never quite reacting as expected, and sometimes causing confusion as a result. Being highly original, they need to ensure that they stay well grounded in material matters and in business concerns. Nervous tension can affect their health adversely, especially the eyes and lower body.

Moon in Aquarius parents are double-sided. They give strong moral support but also expect their children to be independent at a young age.

Stones:
jet

Flower:
snowdrop

Animal:
swallow

Moon in Pisces

People with their moon in Pisces are extremely sensitive, and often psychic, with a natural intuitive ability. Being kind, compassionate and understanding, they are frequently drawn to working in humanitarian occupations, such as nursing, social work and healing.

They also seek out spiritual experiences: because the moon in this placement can make them feel things so deeply, it can lead to lack of confidence and they will try to find ways of reducing their insecurity by means of spiritual or mystical practices. There is also a creative streak in lunar Pisceans, and once they have gained confidence in their abilities, they have the potential to be extremely successful.

They see life as far more than material, and give a great deal to those in need, often at personal cost. However, this moon sign can also be dishonest, not because of any malice, but because of the fear of conflict, and a desire to limit any personal confrontations. Pisces moons can tend to put things off, making all kinds of excuses, but with the right kind of encouragement and positive input, they have the ability to make a great contribution to society.

Being romantic by nature and soft at heart, they do require strong and positive partners, who will understand the Piscean sensitivity and vulnerability, and who will give back as much as they contribute to any partnership. Because of their romanticism it is easy to abuse the goodwill of Piscean moons, or to misunderstand their deep emotional nature.

Pisces moon parents are kind and sensitive to their children's needs, but sometimes lean on them for support. However, they will stand by their children through thick and thin.

Stones:
amethyst

Flower:
mosses

Animal:
fish

ABOVE: *When the moon is passing through Pisces, guard against any excessive emotional outbursts or a tendency to indulge yourself in your feelings, especially any negative or depressive tendencies. Keep things lighthearted, and try to be creative and positive.*

The Lunar Wheel of the Year

I N ARYAN MYTHOLOGY, the moon is the oldest recorded way of measuring time. Ancient civilizations calculated their significant festivals and activities according to the lunar cycles of the year. Our present Gregorian calendar is calculated according to the position of the earth in relation to the sun – measuring the length of a solar day – rather than by the far less predictable monthly cycle of the moon. Although it is more complicated, many cultures, such as Hebrew and Muslim, still have the means to calculate time by the moon. For Buddhists, too, full and new moons are very important times, because they believe that Buddha was born, achieved enlightenment and died during the period of the full moon. They still use a lunar calendar today, and one of their biggest annual festivals, Losar (New Year), begins on the February full moon.

A lunar year is calculated by months rather than days (the moon gives its name to "month") and each month incorporates the new, full, waning and dark aspect of the moon. The length of a lunar month is actually 29 days, 12 hours, 44 minutes and 28 seconds.

Several of our solar festivals were originally lunar festivals, hence their appearance in the lunar wheel of the year. Easter is still calculated according to when a particular full moon falls in the year. The Celtic celebrations of Imbolc (celebrated on 1 February) and Beltane (1 May) were also dedicated to the moon.

Some days are dedicated to moon goddesses. One of Diana's festivals is called the Ides of May, and falls at the time of the May full moon. At this time, women

LEFT: *The Celts marked their festivals from the rising of the moon on the evening before the day of a particular event, and often lit ceremonial fires to honour them.*

Lunar Festivals of the Year

30 November eve	Festival of Hecate: weather
20/21 December eve	Winter Solstice – Celtic festival of the stars: light and life
31 January eve	Imbolc: rejuvenation, fertility
7 February	Festival of Selene
12 February	Festival of Diana
15 March	Festival of Cybele
20 March	Festival of Isis
20 March eve	Festival of Eostre (Easter): fertility
31 March	Festival of all Lunar Goddesses
1 May	Beltane/May Day: fertility, warmth and light
9 May	Festival of Artemis
26–31 May	Diana's Ides of May: fertility, abundance
21 June eve	Festival of Ceridwen
13 August eve	Festival of Hecate: weather and thanksgiving
September full moon eve	Festival of Candles/Harvest moon: crop yield
31 October eve	Festival of Hecate: remembrance of ancestors

would clean and tidy grottos, streams and water holes, and then wash the water over themselves as an act of cleansing and to encourage personal fertility. Diana is also venerated at the Harvest moon. Hecate, a moon goddess of the dark aspect, has her annual festival day on 13 August. This is the time when ancient peoples would call for her blessing on fair weather so that the harvest could be brought in safely.

The moon is honoured in many cultures. Zhong Qiu Jie is an autumnal lunar festival held by the Chinese, when offerings are made and celebrations abound to honour a bountiful harvest.

The lunar cycle is celebrated by pagans in the form of "full moon esbats". These ceremonies involve celebrating the full moon and sharing a feast, after any requests or dedications have been made, to signify the great abundance of the mother aspect of the moon and her ripeness at the full phase, being the most powerfully fertile. In many ancient cultures, torches were lit to direct the rays of the moon down to the earth, to ensure her continued influence upon crops, childbirth, and fair weather.

The Moon's Phases

BEFORE THE ADVENT of calendars, the king (or "moonman") was responsible for watching the moon's cycle and informing the tribal members when the new moon arrived, so that activities associated with the crescent could begin. He would continue to watch throughout the lunar month, informing members of each new phase. Any ceremonies, although led by the tribal chief, were always presided over by women, who were considered the potentizers of the moon's energy.

Traditionally, the moon has four phases: new, full, waning and dark. In ancient civilizations, the moon was considered to have three faces: the crescent, the full and the waning/dark. These three faces were embodied in the maiden, mother and crone of the Triple Goddess.

The New Moon

Associated with Artemis, the new moon heralds the beginning of a new cycle, and is the time in magic when new opportunities can be called for. On the magic circle,

the new moon is placed in the east – the place of the moonrise and the place of a rising dawn. This slender beauty is seen as young and vulnerable, filled with the potential of a full moon to come, but as yet unrealized. The new moon is the maiden, the innocent, the conception, and this is a good time to work on health

LEFT: *Artemis is often shown many-breasted to indicate her ability to nourish and nurture new life.*

ABOVE: *The first quarter of the moon's cycle begins with the new moon, and lasts until half the moon is visible.*

and personal growth, and to put plans into action for the month ahead. The new moon-time lasts for approximately three days of the first quarter.

The first quarter is a time of expansion, development and growth, and can still be used for the same purposes as the new moon, as long as you make sure that you have completed your groundwork.

The way to recognize a new moon is to check that her "horns" are facing to the left. During the first quarter, you will see up to half of the moon's surface illuminated and, again, this will be her right hand side.

The Full Moon

The full moon is the moon at her fullest and ripest. Represented by Isis, Selene, and Diana, amongst others, she is the embodiment of fertility, abundance and illumination. She is the moon at her most powerfully feminine and so is the fruit-bearer, the one who can encourage any seeds to

grow. The full moon can be called upon to give fertility in the fields as well as fertility of the body, and also for safe journeys across water. The most potent time for full-moon magic occurs in the three days prior to a full moon and at the actual time of the full moon. This is the second quarter.

In full-moon ceremonies, the high priestess draws down the energies of a full moon into herself, embodying the great mystery of the feminine, by adopting the pentagram position within a sacred circle she has cast. Having drawn down the energies, she can be filled and refreshed, so that she has the strength to complete the next cycle of events in her life and the life of her community. Having drawn down the moon, the priestess can call for assistance for others, ask for blessings and healings for those in need and empower any of her own wishes.

The full moon is also well known as the time of moon madness, or "lunacy" (from luna, the moon). The powerful energy of a full moon can trigger such things as epilepsy, as well as increasing the potential for accidents. People vulnerable to the influence of the full moon will feel more emotionally or mentally shaky at this time. In the female reproductive cycle, the full moon is the time of ovulation.

The Waning/Dark Moon

This moon is ruled by Hecate – a goddess of magic, sorcery and wisdom – Cybele and Ceridwen. The waning moon is the time when things can be cast away, let go of and released. It is also the time when insights can be gained. This is the power time for healings. Be aware that these goddesses are powerful. The days of the waning moon are called the third quarter (when the left-hand side of the moon is illuminated and the right-hand side is dark). After this period, the moon enters the rising power time of the fourth quarter, the last phase of the lunar cycle. This is a necessary part of the circle of Luna, when things can retreat into themselves, sink back into the earth, and rest for a while before the pull of the new moon draws everything out of itself again.

In sorcery, the dark moon is the time of black magic, especially during the winter months, when the light on the earth is low. However, it is the most potent time for gaining understanding, and should ideally be spent in contemplation, meditation and preparation, seeking the spiritual guidance of Isis, mother goddess of the moon, or

ABOVE: *The waning moon, ruled by Hecate, can be celebrated with candles, dragon charms and hands and feet decorated with red henna.*

of Sophia, holy lady of wisdom. A dark moon is not the time for action unless it is of a banishing nature, and this is best done during the waning moon, the first to fourth day after the full moon, and not on the nights of true darkness, unless you know what you are doing.

Hecate as a goddess of the underworld is symbolized with snakes for hair, like Medusa the Gorgon. She carries a torch and is attended by hounds. Hecate is also the goddess of crossroads, which is possibly why wrongdoers were strung up on gallows that were traditionally erected at crossroads. They were left to Hecate, goddess of the dark moon.

LEFT: *Early Christian women continued the tradition of praying to the moon rather than to God for favours.*

Circle of Luna

This is an approximation of the moon's cycle and her most active times in each quarter.
Read the chart from new moon to new moon.

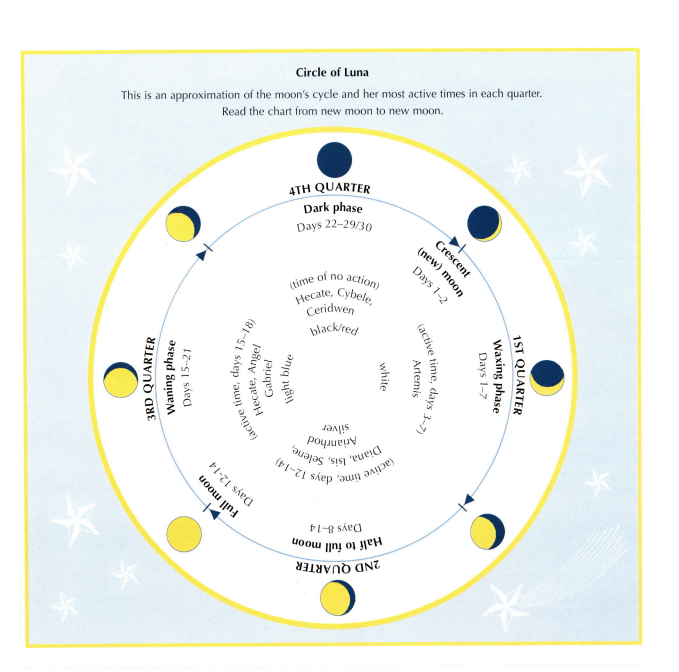

4TH QUARTER

Dark phase

Days 22–29/30

Crescent (new) moon

Days 1–2

1ST QUARTER

Waging phase

Days 1–7

(time of no action)
Hecate, Cybele, Ceridwen

black/red

(active time, days 3–7)
Artemis

white

(active time, days 15–18)
Hecate, Angel Gabriel

light blue

3RD QUARTER

Waning phase

Days 15–21

silver
Arianrhod
Diana, Isis, Selene,
(active time, days 12–14)

Full moon

Days 12–14

Half to full moon

Days 8–14

2ND QUARTER

The Moon and Women

A S THE PROTECTOR and guardian of women, the moon has long been associated with the female reproductive cycle. Many ancient civilizations performed fertility rituals and celebrated the moon at annual festivals dedicated to the goddess, to seek her help and favour with conception.

The female menstrual cycle mirrors the cycle of the moon in duration. The Latin word *mens*, meaning both mind and moon, is the basis for our word menstruation. The time of ovulation is likely to occur during a full moon. Women, the bearers of life, were seen by ancient civilizations as children of the moon goddess. Women can be very powerful, if their deep intuition is blended with spiritual wisdom. The full cycle of Luna must be travelled if wisdom is to be found. This can be achieved quite easily with meditation and devotion to the heart.

Within the heart of all women is the cycle of love. A woman generally finds it easy to nourish and care for others, to devote her life to beauty and harmony, and to speak from feeling rather than intellect. This reflects her "brightmoon" phase. Then there is the part of a woman that is jealous, possessive, scheming, vengeful, malicious, pre-menstrual – her "darkmoon" phase. During their menstruation, women are extremely

ABOVE: *Some ancient civilizations perceived the moon as masculine, and later as hermaphrodite – both male and female. More recently, largely because of changes in our religious structure, she is considered female and is depicted as such in works of art.*

sensitive and highly perceptive. Many ancient civilizations considered them too powerful when they were on their "moontime" and it was common for women to remove themselves from the tribe. Though this is not practised in modern societies, it may still be a good idea to set time aside to go within and use each "moontime" as a time to let go of the past cycle, and to allow the flow to cleanse and take away any problems or difficulties, thus making way for the new.

Once wisdom spills into her heart, a woman passes the highest initiation and the lunar cycle takes on its greater perspective. No longer dictated to by emotions, but rather by insight and discrimination, no longer attached, but rhythmical, no longer selfish or jealous, but unconditionally compassionate, the wise woman has an extraordinary power.

Like women, the moon has cycles. Both of them possess the ability to generate the right conditions for new life and to continue to nurture it.

RIGHT: *A woman is a natural healer. When a child hurts itself, she automatically kisses or rubs it better; when a child cannot sleep, she sings or rocks it rhythmically. The moon and music are intimately linked, as is rhythmical movement (ebb and flow), underlining the correlation between the moon's wisdom and the ability of women to fulfil this role.*

The Moon and the Weather

THE MOON HAS A profound effect upon the earth's climate and atmosphere. She also affects the electromagnetic field that surrounds the earth, creating changes in atmospheric pressure that bring variations in the weather. Continuing research into the moon's effect upon the earth's magnetic field, carried out since the 1960s, has shown that the full moon increases the incidence of meteorites falling to earth, and also affects the amount of ozone in the atmosphere.

The earth's magnetic field changes enough, during the monthly cycle of the moon, to affect not only the weather but our health as well, since human beings are sensitive to magnetism. The old wives' tale of feeling things "in one's bones" can act as a good predictor of rain. Our rheumatic aches and pains can be a valid interpretation of increased dampness in the air. The moon is known to influence rainfall, to raise storms, tidal flows, earthquakes, hurricanes and volcanic eruptions. Increases in these events have all been recorded just after a full moon. This aspect of the moon's power has psychological effects too. Mental instability increases dramatically during any very unsettled or stormy weather.

In severe drought, tribal people would make an offering of precious water to the moon, or milk a cow and offer the fluid in her honour. Clay balls were often flung at the full moon to encourage rain (clay being excellent at retaining water).

RIGHT: *If you see a single halo around a full moon, you can expect mild breezes; the more halos to be seen, the greater the increase in the wind. Volcanic eruptions frequently occur just after a full moon.*

Foretelling the Weather

★ Moon lore states that a new moon always brings a change in the weather, and if the horns of the moon are sharp it indicates windy weather.

★ A crescent moon cupped and on its back means rain will fall.

★ If you can see a star close to the moon, you can expect to have "wild weather".

★ A bright full moon heralds good weather and a mottled full moon will bring rain.

The Blue Moon

THE OLD SAYING "once in a blue moon" refers to a time when two moons occur in the same calendar month, a rather rare occurrence. During the twentieth century, for example, there have been only 40 blue moons. A blue moon appears about every two and a half years, usually during a month that has 31 days in it. It signifies a special time: a doubling of the moon's powers during the month that she appears. Considered unlucky by some, the blue moon is, in fact, a magical moon, when long-term objectives can be set. So, a blue moon can be used to sow seeds for your future, giving them time to germinate and grow until the next blue moon rises. But you should be careful if you intend to weave magic during a blue moon. Be very clear about what you ask for, because this moon will be potent, doubling your wish and intent.

ABOVE: *Check for two moons in one month in a lunar calendar, the second moon is the blue moon and is twice as potent as a normal full moon.*

People born during a blue moon have great potential, but may have difficulty bringing their gifts into action. Their strengths are also their weaknesses, and blue moon people have to learn how to harness their powers for the benefit of themselves and those they meet in life.

A blue moon increases the lunar influence on the weather, with a high probability that rainfall, storms and exceptional tides will be more prevalent than usual during that month.

ABOVE: *Because of the power she brings to those born during this time, the blue moon's magic needs to be understood. They may have a tendency to moodiness, volatility and emotionalism, as well as the gentler attributes of compassion, caring, sensitivity and natural intuition.*

Lunar Gardening

B ECAUSE THE MOON has such a strong influence over crop yields, for hundreds of years farmers, agriculturists and gardeners have all used the lunar phases when planting, tending and harvesting crops. This is done by observing the correct phase of the moon for a particular activity, and also by adhering to the sign of the zodiac that it is passing through.

There are four lunar phases to be considered. The moon is increasing in influence between the new and full phases (brightmoon) and decreasing in influence between the waning and dark phases (darkmoon). As a general rule, the first and second quarter are the most auspicious time for planting and tending cereal crops, leafy crops and annual plants and flowers. The third quarter is good for root crops and bulbs, trees, shrubs and rhubarb. The fourth quarter is the best time for garden maintenance: for weeding, cultivation and the removal of pests, especially when the moon is in Aries, Gemini, Leo, or Aquarius. Start a compost heap during the darkmoon time, or harvest and dry herbs and everlasting flowers, especially if the moon is in a fire sign. A water moon is

ABOVE: *Plant sweetcorn during the new moon to encourage fleshy corns.*

the best time to irrigate fields and gardens. If, to begin with, you find it a little too complicated to check the zodiac signs for your gardening tasks, you can simply follow the moon's phases of waxing and waning.

New Moon

Seeds of plants that flower above the ground should be sown at the new moon. This is also the time for farmers to sow cereals such as barley, and for the garden to be planted with asparagus, broccoli, Brussels sprouts, sweetcorn, cabbage, melons, cauliflower, celery, courgettes, cress, horseradish, kohlrabi, leeks, peas, peppers, parsley, spinach, squash and tomatoes. This is also the time for fertilizing and feeding anything that you wish to flourish.

ABOVE: *Bulbs, root crops, perennials and biennials should be tended and planted during the darkmoon phase.*

LEFT: *Lunar gardening doesn't mean gardening by night but rather by her phases through the month.*

Full Moon

Around the full moon is the time to plant watery or fleshy plants like marrows and cucumbers. The moon is at her most influential at this time over the water element. This is also a good time for harvesting the leaves, stems, or seeds of herbs for drying, especially

when the moon is transiting a fire sign. It is important to pick your herbs on a dry day, so that the parts to be harvested will not rot when stored. The best time to harvest is just before midday. String the stems together and hang them upside down in an airy, cool but dry atmosphere, until ready for use.

Pick mushrooms at the full moon. The best time is just after dawn, when the dew is still on the grass. Take them home and have them for breakfast. Do remember that some fungi are poisonous: be very careful to ensure that you pick only edible mushrooms. Get an expert to guide you or consult a good reference book and do not eat anything you are unsure about.

Elemental Gardening table

Gardening by the moon's phases is very simple once you have mastered the basic principles. Just ensure that you are within the correct moon phase for a particular gardening task, and that the moon is passing through an appropriate sign. For details on the moon's phases and when it is passing through a particular star sign, you will need to refer to a lunar almanac. Then check the chart below to discover which zodiacal sign is most appropriate for each activity.

AIR	WATER
Gemini (barren and dry) *Weeding, clearing, pest control*	**Cancer (very fruitful and moist)** *Best sign for planting, sowing and cultivating*
Libra (moist) *Plant fruit trees, fleshy vegetables, root vegetables*	**Scorpio (very fruitful and moist)** *Very good sign for planting, sowing and general cultivation, especially vine fruits; start a compost heap*
Aquarius (barren and dry) *Garden maintenance, weeding and pest control*	**Pisces (very fruitful and moist)** *Excellent for planting, especially root crops*
FIRE	**EARTH**
Aries (barren and dry) *Weeding, clearing, garden maintenance*	**Taurus (fertile and moist)** *Plant root crops and leafy vegetables*
Leo (barren and dry) *Bonfires, ground clearance, weeding*	**Virgo (barren and moist)** *Cultivation, weeding and pest control*
Sagittarius (barren and dry) *Plant onions, garden maintenance*	**Capricorn (productive and dry)** *Good for root vegetables*

ABOVE: *Plant, feed and prune flowers, especially biennials and perennials, during the darkmoon phase.*

Incidentally, the full moon is also an excellent time for baking bread. The influence of the full moon proves the yeast better, and encourages the dough to rise.

Waning and Dark Moon

The waning moon is the time in the moon's cycle for root vegetables, peas and beans, and garlic. Anything undertaken during this time will benefit underground development or retard growth. This is therefore an excellent time to mow the grass, when its return growth will be slowed, or to plough and turn the soil. Gather and harvest crops during the waning moon, especially in late summer, the traditional harvest time. This is an excellent time to prune trees, roses and shrubs, and to water the garden. Making jams and pickles should also be done during a waning moon, for best results.

Crops that are suited to planting during the waning moon are endive, carrots, garlic, onions, potatoes, radishes, beetroot and strawberries.

All flowering bulbs, biennials, and perennials should be planted during this time, especially when the moon is in a water sign. Saplings also benefit from being planted during the waning moon, when she is in Cancer, Scorpio, Pisces or Virgo.

The principles of lunar gardening take a while to adjust to, but after a while, you will find that your flowers bloom brighter, crops grow more succulent and flavoursome, and trees have stronger roots. In fact your whole garden will benefit from this ancient way of gardening.

ABOVE: *Harvesting your vegetables should be done during a waning or dark moon.*

ABOVE: *Radishes, carrots and other roots should be planted during a waning moon.*

ABOVE: *Farmers should concentrate on cereal crops during the brightmoon phase.*

A Water Garden Feature

 IANA'S FESTIVAL DAYS fall upon the May and September full moons. At one of these times, you may like to perform a water ceremony in your garden or at a local waterfall, well, stream, lake or river, or on the seashore. This idea is inspired by the ancient art of well-dressing, when communities "dress" their local source of water with a plaque decorated with symbols, flowers, corn, rice, stones and twigs, placing it by the water as a way of giving thanks. This is an excellent group activity and can be great fun to do with children. Any lunar totem can be included in the design, such as a dove, cat, or owl, or perhaps some circles and spirals.

Perform the ceremony two days before the full moon. As you place your plaque next to the water, you may like to say a prayer to the moon, asking for her blessing and protection for the year to come. Use your own words, as they come.

You will need

- potter's clay
- rolling pin
- piece of wood cut to shape
- knife
- stick or skewer
- flower petals, leaves, twigs, corn, rice, pasta, shells and pebbles
- toothpick (optional)
- wet cloth

1 Roll out the clay to about 6 mm/¼ in. Trace around your chosen wooden shape and cut it out from the clay with the knife.

2 Press the clay down firmly on to the wood, then mark out your design on the surface.

3 Fill in the design using petals, leaves and other elements, pushing them into the clay with your fingernails or a toothpick. Cover your work with a wet cloth when you are not working on it to keep the clay soft.

Lunar Plants

THE MOON, like the planets, has particular plants that come under her influence. These have been used in ceremonies and rituals to the moon goddess, and were also depicted in traditional art and sculpture. Flowers of the moon include all the aquatic plants like water lilies, seaweed, lotus and watercress, as well as jasmine and poppy. All flowers that are white or that blossom at night, such as night-scented stock, come under the regulation of the moon.

Trees associated with the moon include the willow, a tree that thrives near water, the aspen, eucalyptus, pear, plum and lemon. The willow is also known as the

LEFT: *On the night of the new or full moon, you may like to arrange a vase of moon flowers and light two white (new moon) or silver (full moon) candles.*

LEFT: *Make a magical wand from a branch of willow, the moon's wishing tree.*

moon's wishing tree. Calling for favour with a willow tree by tying white, silver or light-blue ribbons to her branches on lunar festival days can help to draw attention to a wish.

Another moon tree is sandalwood. Associated with protection, purification and healing, chippings of the bark of *Santalum album* are used in ceremonies requiring these qualities. It has a beautifully calming and soothing smell.

Camphor is a white resinous gum, extracted from *Cinnamonium camphora*, a tree found in China, Japan and other parts of east Asia. It is one of the aromatic fragrances associated with the moon. Camphor has a strong and distinct smell, and has cooling qualities rather like menthol. Camphor's cool and yet penetrating property brings it close to the lunar mysteries. By strewing it on the ground, or burning it ritually, people of the ancient world felt they were able to attract the favours and attentions of the goddess.

The Moon and Numerology

IN NUMEROLOGY the moon is associated with the number two, a highly feminine number, although in magic she is assigned the number nine. Any years or months that add up to the number two will come under the influence of the moon. Moon years are romantic, creative, unpredictable, deep and intuitive, with a need to bring harmony and stability. However, if the negative aspects of the moon prevail during a number two year, there will be a tendency for depression, cruelty, and possessiveness.

To discover if you are in a moon year, take the four figures and add them together. (For example, the year 2090 becomes 2 + 9 = 11; 1 + 1 = 2.)

Leading up to the new millennium, the year 1999, when broken down into a single number, becomes the number one (1 + 9 + 9 + 9 = 28; 2 + 8 =10; 1 + 0 = 1). The sun is represented by 1.

The year 2000, however, adds up to the number two. Thus, being a lunar year, it heralds an important time to get in touch with inner feelings and emotions, to be with the family, to enhance productivity, and to promote the good of the whole. As the wheel of time turns from sun to moon, so the less predictable but fruitful moon holds sway.

Moon people (those whose name or date of birth adds up to the number two) are dedicated parents, have a need for security and emotional reassurance, and have close links with nature and water, in a positive or negative way. Darker aspects of this personality include jealousy, manipulation, deception and vindictiveness. "Two" people need to guard against being two-faced.

1	2	3	4	5	6	7	8	9
A	B	C	D	E	F	G	H	I
J	K	L	M	N	O	P	Q	R
S	T	U	V	W	X	Y	Z	

ABOVE: *The strongest lunar influence will be felt by the individual whose birth date adds up to the number two.*

LEFT: *The lunar name will play a less significant part but will still affect the qualities of a personality.*

Turning Names into Numbers

To discover if you are a moon person, take the letters of your chosen name or your birth date and translate them into numbers using this chart. This can be done with either your full name, your first name or a chosen name that you use in place of your given name. "Sarah", for example, becomes 20 (1 + 1 + 9 + 1 + 8 = 20; 2 + 0 = 2). Sarahs will feel a strong connection with the attributes of the moon. To work out if you are a moon child, add up the numbers of your full birth date (for example, 2.4.1967 becomes 29: 2 + 9 = 11, 1 + 1 = 2).

Lunar Colours

L IKE THE PLANETS in our solar system, the moon has colours that are traditionally associated with her. Use and wear the appropriate lunar colours when you are performing ceremonies during the various phases of the moon, or simply to maintain your connection with the moon's phases and increase your awareness of her cycles and influence.

White has always been associated with purity and innocence and therefore represents the crescent or new moon. White and milky stones, like the moonstone, opal or milky quartz, are also associated with the new moon. White candles should be burned when working during this phase – for example, to call for new opportunities.

Silver, both as a colour and as a metal, has the most favourable lunar associations, because of its coolness and fluidity. Silver jewellery, especially when worn during the new- to full-moon phase, can enhance all the magical qualities of the moon and help to connect the intuitive self with lunar energies.

LEFT: Burn two silver candles when working with general moon magic, such as a full moon celebration, or esbats, as they are known in pagan circles.

Light blue has long been associated with the Virgin Mary, a lady of the moon, and is a very healing colour. It can soothe, calm and cool heated emotions, illness or burns and stings. Once appropriate medical attention has

LEFT: White stones and flowers will increase your connection to the new or crescent moon. Lilies are particularly linked to the moon. Burn some white candles when performing any lunar ceremonies in this phase.

LEFT: Float three, seven or nine light-blue candles in a clear glass bowl filled with spring water for healing ceremonies and during the waning moon.

ABOVE: *Black and red are the colours of the darkmoon goddesses. Although traditionally described as the time for dark magic, it is also the peak time for women to connect to their innate wisdom.*

been administered, visualize a light-blue colour bathing a specific area, or the whole person, and you will notice a marked reduction in the symptoms.

Black is a much maligned colour in some quarters. This is the colour of the darkmoon, when the inner world can speak most clearly. It is associated with Hecate, goddess of death and the underworld. Black is a silent, inward colour, so can be worn as protection or when seeking insight. It is the colour of power and identity. Burn white candles during the darkmoon phase, and meditate in black clothes or cloaked in a black cloth to help you travel inwards.

Traditionally, red is put with the full moon, but here it is placed with the dark moon because red has not only long been associated with the underworld but also represents the female. In the cycle of Luna, menstruation would occur during the waning/darktime of the moon.

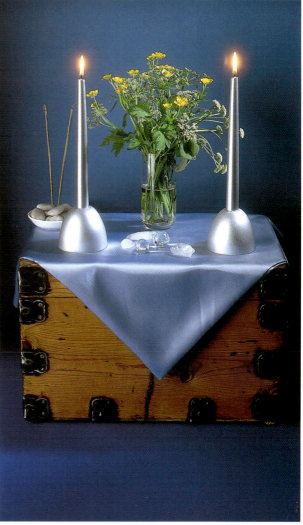

ABOVE: *If you feel drawn to setting up an altar to the full moon, you may like to use a light-blue cloth, silver candles, sandalwood incense and wild water meadow or riverside flowers, adding any other lunar totems and crystals you wish. Remember to be careful of poisonous plants and not to pick protected species.*

The Moon and the Tarot

T AROT CARDS are believed to have originated in Egypt although, like most inherited systems of divination, we cannot be certain of their real origin. In medieval times, the moon was depicted as Fortuna, the Wheel of Fortune in the tarot deck. This card depicts the ups and downs of life, the cycles that represent life's changing fortunes, sometimes hard and sometimes easy. Like the Wheel of Fortune, the moon is ever-changing, and reminds us that life ebbs and flows.

The moon card in the tarot deck is numbered 18 (1 + 8). This gives the number nine, which is the magical number of the moon. Nine denotes the completion of a cycle and so signifies that a new beginning is about to occur. When you draw this card, it tells you that intuition and perception will be your greatest allies in the days to come. Trust in your feelings, and take a little time before making decisions of a life-changing nature.

LEFT: The tarot can be a very powerful means of connecting with the intuitive forces of the moon, acting as a focus of attention for perception to unfold.

BELOW: The moon in the tarot traditionally symbolizes deception, fear, and uncertainty, often found in a spread where someone is having (or thinking of having) a secret affair. It can also indicate that an important change is about to occur.

This is a card of feelings and emotions, of all aspects of the feminine, and so may represent an emotional or psychic understanding or change, especially if time is spent in contemplation of the moon's present message. It also conveys a warning that emotionalism and negative reactions that are not tempered with any higher wisdom can lead you into emotional confusion. This card signifies that you are completing one cycle and not yet beginning another – so can raise fears, doubts, and upsets. Don't get carried away with fantasies; stay practical and well grounded in reality, and trust that as one door closes, so another opens.

Take the moon card from the deck and hold it so that the picture is touching your third eye (in the centre of your forehead). Close your eyes and melt into the card, noting symbols, images and feelings that arise.

Making a Lunar Tarot Card

One way to deepen your connection with the moon is to make your own lunar card. This can be done with paints, crayons, collage or any medium you want to work in. Make up a design of your own that represents the moon for you, just sit quietly with paper and pencil and allow the ideas to form. When your moon card is completed, you can place it upon your altar, and meditate upon it, to help to bring insights and revelations. If you feel you cannot draw, cut out pictures and glue them to the card instead. Make the card just before the new moon, to ensure that your intuition and perception increase as the new moon grows.

You will need

- scissors
- white card
- ruler
- silver pen
- paints or crayons
- paintbrush
- glue
- a selection of the following: silver glitter, silver and/or blue sequins, stars and moon sequin shapes
- pictures of moon animals, birds, trees, crystals, moon flowers, water
- white feathers (especially dove or duck)
- blue ribbons
- silver tape
- blue or silver candles
- matches

1 Cut out a piece of card measuring 9 x 13 cm/ 3½ x 5 in and draw your chosen design on it. You can make the card bigger if you feel confident to do so.

2 Paint your design or glue on your chosen collage materials. Let your mind be led by imagination and creativity as you make up your design.

3 When it is complete, place the card on your altar or special area. Light two blue or silver candles. Meditate upon the images for three nights. Make a note of any unusual dreams.

A Lunar Talisman

IN MAGIC, the moon is associated with the number nine. The "kamea", or magic square, of the moon adds up to the number nine in all directions and can be used in magic to connect with the powers and gifts that the moon provides.

When making a lunar talisman, it is important to observe the correct timing: the new moon to the full moon is the time for drawing things to you, and the full moon to the beginning of the dark moon is the time for releasing things. For example, if you are seeking new beginnings or fertility, use the new moon, and if you are asking for healing, use the waning time. The new to full phase is for growth and attraction. The waning to dark phase is for decrease and removal.

Place an attracting talisman in the light of the moon with a moonstone or white circular stone on top, until your wish is granted. Take a releasing talisman to a river or seashore on the first night after a full moon and place it in the water to be taken away. Watch it leave, and then turn away. Do not look back.

To make your talisman, you will first need to work out the sigil of your name. Convert your name into numerals using the Numerology Chart on page 47. For example, the name Isabel becomes the numbers 911253. Then trace the shape of those numbers on the kamea. Begin with a small circle, then draw a line connecting the numerals until you have a sigil, or pattern. Isabel would begin by joining nine to one, then one to two and so on. End the sigil with a line.

The Kamea of the Moon

A lunar kamea can be used to balance the emotions, to call for fertility, and to enhance perceptions and psychic abilities, as well as for journeys at night or over water.

37	78	29	70	21	62	13	54	5
6	38	79	30	71	22	63	14	46
47	7	39	80	31	72	23	55	15
16	48	8	40	81	32	64	24	56
57	17	48	9	41	73	33	65	25
26	58	18	50	1	42	74	34	66
67	27	59	10	51	2	43	75	35
36	68	19	60	11	52	3	44	76
77	28	69	20	61	12	53	4	45

37	78	29	70	21	62	13	54	5
6	38	79	30	71	22	63	14	46
47	7	39	80	31	72	23	55	15
16	48	8	40	81	32	64	24	56
57	17	48	9	41	73	33	65	25
26	58	18	50	1	42	74	34	66
67	27	59	10	51	2	43	75	35
36	68	19	60	11	52	3	44	76
77	28	69	20	61	12	53	4	45

LEFT:
Whenever your sigil runs consecutively through one number represent this with a loop.

Making a Lunar Talisman

A talisman is simply a written wish, and can take any form. This lunar talisman will call upon the power of the moon.

You will need

- 2 silver or white candles
- matches
- silver pen
- ruler
- 23 cm/9 in square of natural paper

1 Light your two silver or white candles, saying as you do so:
"Hail to you Levanah. I light these candles in your honour and ask for your assistance this night."

ABOVE: *Make your talisman on a Monday, the day of the moon, preferably after she has risen and during the correct phase for attracting or releasing.*

2 Draw a 5 cm/2 in square in the top left hand corner of the piece of paper. Copy the sigil of your name (do not include any numbers) into the square. Write your wish (for a safe journey, for example) in the remaining space.

3 Fold the four corners of the paper into the centre to make a diamond shape, then repeat twice more.

RIGHT: *Leave your talisman with a moonstone in the light of the increasing moon to draw her favour to your wish.*

Moon Crystals

T HE MOON HAS been worshipped and associated with particular sacred stones for thousands of years. Traditionally, white stones are associated with the waxing and full moon, and black or dark stones with the waning and dark aspects.

Certain crystals have a sympathetic resonance with the cool, subtle energies of the moon. These crystals can help to align your vibrations to hers, so inducing clearer dreams, clairvoyant awakening, deeper perceptions and emotional understanding. Some moon crystals have a balancing effect upon the menstrual cycle, some upon dreaming and yet others upon emotional health.

BRIGHT MOONTIME CRYSTALS

White, clear or watery bright stones should be used for the new to full phase of the lunar cycle.

ABOVE: *You can take your crystals to lakes or the seashore during a full moon and cleanse them there in the water.*

Celestite

In its blue or white varieties, celestite can help to link you to your spirit guides, to the beings of the light who help to illuminate your way in the dreamtime, so that gifts from the spirit can be given to you.

Moonstone

A moonstone crystal can be used to balance the hormonal cycle, calm any unsettled emotions, especially over parenting issues, and induce lucid dreaming.

Aquamarine

An icy blue crystal, aquamarine makes an ideal dream crystal, tuning you into the rhythms of the sea and the depths of your own spirit, so that you can access divine wisdom and guidance.

Circular white stones

As well as particular gems or crystals, any round white-coloured stones or pebbles can be used to represent the full moon, or increase your connections with her.

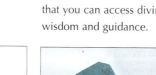

Azurite (right)

Known as the "stone of heaven", azurite can help attune your mind to the psychic world. It ranges in colour from dark blue to light blue, one of the lunar colours.

Clear quartz (right)

A crystal that looks like frozen water, clear quartz has a strong affinity with the moon and can be used to enhance and direct the moon's rays in ceremonies of healing or invocation.

Pearl (below)

"Pearls of wisdom" are spoken of in the Bible. Pearls are symbolic of the moon because they are made in the sea. They represent purity, clarity and grace, and can be used to help enhance those qualities. The wearer is healthy if the pearls hold their soft sheen. Pearl flower essence can be used to balance the hormones and emotions, and to increase confidence in inner wisdom.

RIGHT: Leave lunar crystals out for three days prior to a full moon to re-energize them with lunar powers.

DARK MOONTIME CRYSTALS

Black, dark or cloudy stones are used to represent this phase of the moon's cycle. This is the time when insights can be gained, wisdom can be sought, and preparation made for the new moonrise.

Holy flint (right)

A flint with a hole in it can protect the wearer from night terrors, fears from negative thought forms. String one on a red thread and wear or carry it with you wherever you need to.

Jet

A deeply black mineral, formed from fossilized timber, jet is highly symbolic of the dark moon. Jet calms all the subtle bodies, clears a heavy head, and can help in the lifting of depression or gloominess. It is especially useful for clearing negative inner or outer environments where the build-up of tension is preventing sleep.

Citrine

Actually a crystal of the sun, because of its vibrant amber colour, citrine has been included here as a

preventer of nightmares and night fears. It warms and soothes the mental and emotional body, so that you feel calm and relaxed enough to have a good night's sleep. Citrine can help to soothe children back to sleep.

Black stones

Circular black or dark stones have also traditionally been associated with and used during the dark moon phase. Keep an eye out for them on riverside or beach walks and then carry them with you whenever you are feeling confused or disorientated, as they will help to bring illumination.

Caring for Your Crystals

Crystals have the ability to attract, store or direct energy. If your crystal feels heavy, full and dull put it out on the night of a full moon and leave for four days so that it takes in some of the waning moon. This helps it to release excess energies. If the crystal feels empty and lifeless put it out in the new moon to help it restore its vitality. To find out what your crystal needs, sit with it quietly and you will sense what is the right thing to do.

There are various ways to clean crystals. The best one for lunar crystals is to hold the stones under running water then leave in moonlight to dry. You can also cleanse a crystal in the smoke from an incense or smudge stick, or use visualization by blowing over the stones as you imagine clearing the negatives, or bury the stones in the earth and leave for four days.

Casting a Brightmoon Circle

THIS CEREMONY CAN BE PERFORMED every month to honour the moon, as the protector and guardian of women. When women cast the circle it will refresh and rejuvenate them for the month to come, for a man it will have a symbolic rather than biological significance as he follows his own rhythms and cycles from the female within. The ceremony can be done outdoors or in, within two days leading up to a full moon.

You will need

- 13 circular stones, river stones or moon crystals
- salt
- aromatherapy burner
- matches
- jasmine essential oil
- 9 candles

1 Turning clockwise, lay down 12 of your chosen stones (these can be all different sizes) in a circle around you, beginning in the south. Place the last stone in the centre.

2 Sprinkle the stones with some salt. Light the burner and put in three drops of jasmine oil.

3 Place eight candles around the circle and one by the centre stone. As you light the candles, say,
"Magna Dei, light of the night, I light these candles to guide your moonrays here. I ask you to come and bless this circle."

4 Facing south, stand with your arms outstretched above your head and your feet quite wide apart. Reach towards the sky. Say the lunar invocation:
"Hail to thee Sophia, holy spirit of the wisemoon. I call upon you to enter and fill me with your light. Protect me and guide me on the moonway. Teach me your wisdom and truth as I seek your clarity and guidance."

5 Imagine yourself drawing down the powers of the moon into yourself. Allow yourself to be refreshed and re-filled with the feminine virtues of wisdom, beauty and grace. Let the moon bless your feelings and perceptions until you feel energized and content. Bring your arms down to your sides. Close your circle by saying *"Thank you"*. Blow out your candles and dispose of organic ingredients outside.

Moon Medicines

MOTHER MOON HOLDS important healing energies that can be called upon during her various phases: the new moon for health, vitality and regeneration; the full moon for fertility; the waning phase to remove the symptoms and ailments associated with general health problems. It is important to stress here that if you do have a concern about your health, you should consult a qualified medical practitioner.

Lunar medicine is made utilizing the light of either a new, full or a waning moon. Being the mother figure of humankind, the moon can empower medicines with healing and calming vibrations.

Timing is important, so make sure the moon is in the correct phase before you begin. You may find you have to wait a while for the correct phase of the moon's cycle, but please do stick to the guidelines outlined above. This will ensure that your medicine will contain the most appropriate vibrations for your needs.

RIGHT: It is advisable to only make outdoor lunar medicines when the weather is clear and calm outside.

Moon Dew Medicine

You can take moonstone flower essence to help to balance your menstrual cycle, following the instructions on the bottle.

Another beautiful attribute of the moon is her connection with fertility. In ancient days, women would rise before dawn and go to the fields on the day of the full moon to bathe in the early morning moon dew. Washing down their bodies with the moisture of the early morning, they would call to Luna for her favours, either for a child or for fertile crops.

To bathe in moon dew yourself, all you need to do is to rise before dawn and go to a field or into the garden. Gather some dew into your hands by scraping them over the grasses and flowers and wipe down your face, hands and feet. If you have enough privacy you may like to bathe your whole body. While washing, feel the moon caressing your skin, and the feminine influences permeating your body. Call to Mother Moon to bless and protect you, and ask her for what you need. Once you have finished your request or prayer, say thank you to her.

Lunar Medicine to Reduce Stress

To make a moon medicine that is helpful in times of emotional strain, you will need to perform this healing ceremony three nights after the first night of a full moon, after sunset. It can be performed outside on a calm night, or inside by the light of the moon, by an open window, for example.

You will need
- glass bowl
- 9 white nightlights
- matches
- moonstone
- spring water

1 Place the glass bowl on the floor in front of you, then position the nine nightlights in a circle around it.

2 Light the candles, starting with the one in the south, saying while you do so:
"Hail to thee Levanah, Queen of Heaven. I call for your blessings and ask that your moonrays fill this essence with healing."

3 Put your crystal in the bowl and pour in the spring water until the crystal is completely covered. Leave it in place for at least three hours. Do not leave the nightlights burning unattended and replace any that burn out.

4 After three hours, blow out the nightlights, remove the crystal, pour the infusion into a glass and sip slowly while visualizing yourself being touched by the moon's gentle rays.

Psychic Dreams

YOU CAN enhance your connection to the inner world of dreams by using an aquamarine crystal placed under your pillow as you sleep.

Aquamarine crystals are quite easily obtainable from crystal suppliers and some new age shops. Store your dream crystal in a little pouch, made from a shimmery material in pale blue or silver and decorated with moon charms and sequins. Perform a dedication ceremony on the crystal before using it.

MAKING A CRYSTAL POUCH

You will need
- 7.5 x 20 cm/3 x 8 in piece of fabric
- needle and cotton thread
- silver crescent or full moon charm
- sequins in silver, blue and green
- small safety pin
- 2 x 20 cm/8 in lengths of thin blue or silver ribbon
- aquamarine crystal

1 To make the pouch, turn in and sew a narrow hem along both long edges on the wrong side of the fabric.

2 Sew your moon decorations and sequins on to the right side. Turn down a double 1 cm/½ in hem along the short edges, making a casing for the ribbon.

3 Fold the fabric in half, right sides together, and sew along the two long edges until you reach the casing. Leave the casing unsewn. Turn right sides out. Using a safety pin, thread one piece of ribbon through both sides of the casing and back to the starting point. Knot the ends. Repeat from the other side.

Awakening the Psychic

To empower your dreamtime with the moon's energies, place any moon-governed offering by the side of your bed, as an exchange for her help. This can be seashells, river stones, moon charms, or moon flowers for example, and then dedicate them to her with a personal prayer. This can be done on a monthly basis. If using flowers as your offering ensure you dispose of them with thanks and sensitivity.

DEDICATING YOUR CRYSTAL

Aquamarine is ideal to help develop psychic connections, but before you do this you can clear your dreamtime by first placing jet or citrine in your pouch. Place this under your pillow for a few nights during a waning moon until any nightmares or unsettled sleep patterns you may have been suffering from are gone.

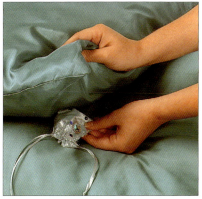

1 For your ceremony, choose a clear, calm night, just before or during the full-moon phase, especially when the moon is in a water sign (Cancer, Pisces or Scorpio). Dedicate your crystal just after sunset when the moon is visible to you indoors.

2 Hold the crystal up to the light of the moon, saying as you do so: *"Hail to thee Levanah. I call to you to bring your blessings to this moon crystal, and ask you to fill it with your rays, that I may learn the wisdom of the dreamtime. Thank you."*

3 Place your crystal in your dream pouch. Put it under your pillow for one month. Perceptive dreams should then enter your sleep. You can perform this ceremony of dedication for your dream crystal every month at the full moon if you like, or every three months as a matter of course.

The Sacred Moon Tree

T HIS MYTHICAL TREE is a "tree of the gods", said to provide the fruits of immortality. The secrets of immortality are held by the moon rather than the sun, because she has the power over life, death and regeneration, owing to her influence on rhythms and cycles, as well as conception and germination. The sacred tree of the gods is therefore placed in her domain.

Past civilizations believed that the fruits of immortality actually grew upon this sacred tree on the moon, and ceremonies were ritually performed by Vedic priests of India, using an intoxicating milky juice extracted from the Soma plant, *Asclepias acida*. Soma was also the name of a Vedic god, equivalent to the Roman god Bacchus, and so strong is the link with the moon that in post-Vedic writings, Soma is the name given to the moon itself.

Soma is known as the king of plants, because of its powerful link with the gods. By taking Soma, the holy people would also be able to connect with the deeper aspects of lunar wisdom, the wisdom that comes from deep within the psyche, and is innately feminine.

Female Wisdom

All women can relate to the feeling of "knowing" something about a future event, or of having strong gut feelings about a particular issue. Men can work on this feminine side of their personalities too by deepening the bond with the moon and honouring her presence in the night sky, especially when she is full.

The highest initiation of Luna is one of wisdom, of allowing the psyche to influence action and to follow this inner voice. The great Wise Mother, beyond death, beyond the veil of illusion, holds these secrets of feminine spirituality. Soma from the sacred Moon Tree, therefore, represents both immortality and profound wisdom.

ABOVE: *Developing lunar awareness will help to increase trust in the more subtle aspects of the psyche, including perception, intuition and psychic understanding.*

Index and Acknowledgements

angels, 14
animal totems, 16–19
aquamarine, 54, 60–1
Aquarius, 30
Arianrhod, 13, 17
Aries, 20
Artemis, 12, 13, 17, 33, 34, 17
Aztecs, 10
azurite, 55

bears, 17
blue moon, 41
brightmoon circle, 57

camphor, 46
Cancer, 23
Capricorn, 29
cats, 17
celestite, 54
Ceridwen, 17, 33
citrine, 56
colours, 48–9
cows, 18

crescent moon, 8, 34
crystals, 54–6, 60–1
Cybele, 13, 17, 33

dark moon, 34, 42, 44
Diana, 12, 13, 17, 32–3, 34, 45, 17, 19
dreams, 17, 60–1, 19

Easter, 32, 33
eclipses, 17
Egypt, 12, 17, 18
Eostre, 16, 33

fertility, 16, 18, 34–5, 38, 58
festivals, 11, 32–3, 38
flint, 56
flowers, 46
foxes, 17
frogs, 17
full moon, 8, 12, 34–5, 38, 40, 42, 43–4

Gabriel, 14
Galileo, 8
gardening, 42–5
Gemini, 22
Gnostics, 12

hares, 16
healing, 14–15, 58
Hecate, 12, 13, 17, 18, 33
Isis, 12–13, 17, 18, 33, 34

jet, 56

legends, 10–11
Leo, 24
Libra, 26
lions, 11, 17
lunacy, 35
lunar cycles, 32–3

Ma'at, 12
Mayan culture, 10
medicines, 58–9
menstrual cycle, 12, 35, 38
mirrors, 11
moon dew, 58
moonstone, 54
myths, 10–11

Native Americans, 10–11, 16, 17, 18, 19
new moon, 8, 12, 34, 42
numerology, 47, 52

orbit, moon's, 8
owls, 18

pearls, 55
phases of the moon, 12, 34–5, 42
Pisces, 31

quartz, 55

sacred moon tree, 62–3
Sagittarius, 28

sandalwood, 46
Scorpio, 27
Selene, 12, 13, 17, 33, 34
snails, 11
Soma, 62
Sophia, 12, 13
spiders, 10–11
Sumerians, 10
superstitions, 11

talisman, lunar, 52–3
tarot cards, 50–1
Taurus, 21
Thoth, 12
toads, 17
totems, animal, 16–19
trees, 46, 62–3
Triple Goddess, 13, 34
Ur, 10

Venus, 12
Virgin Mary, 13, 14, 48
Virgo, 25

water garden, 45
weather, 40
wolves, 16
women, 38–9

Thanks to the following picture libraries and photographers for the use of their pictures:
AKG: 11tl; 13r; 14l; 19t; 20; 21; 22; 23; 24; 25; 26; 27; 28; 29; 30; 31.
BBC Natural History Unit: 17br (Lynne M. Stone); 18br (Artur Tabor); 19tl (Pete Oxford); 32 (Martin Dohrn).
A-Z Botanical: 42t; 44br, bl, bm, t.
Bridgeman Art Library: 11br; 12t, br, l; 14r; 36bl; 39; 50bl. e. t. archive: 8bl; 10bl, tr; 13tl; 34bl.
Mary Evans Picture Library: 33.
Fine Art Photographic: 38; 61tl.
The Garden Picture Library: 42b.
Images Colour Library: 6; 9; 18tr; 34tr; 41l; 47; 53tr; 62.
Tony Stone Images: 1; 7; 8tr; 16l, r; 17l; 19br; 35; 36bl; 40; 41r; 54tr; 58tr; 60br.

MAKING A MOON TREE

You can make and decorate your own moon tree during the period coming up to and during the full moon phase. You might like to make one for Christmas one year, in place of the traditional evergreen tree.

Our traditional Christmas tree is hung with baubles to represent the planets continuing to encircle the earth throughout the coming year. This moon tree has been decorated with fairy lights to represent the stars of the lunar sky, to ensure heavenly blessings.

You will need

- branched willow or aspen bough
- silver spray paint
- pot or container
- river stones
- clear glass fairy lights (optional)
- silver totems
- white cotton thread
- thin blue ribbons
- silver crescents
- light blue, silver and/or white baubles
- seashells
- white or pastel paper or silk flowers
- 2 white candles
- matches

1 Spray your branch with silver paint and leave it to dry completely.

2 Stand the branch in a container and fill in around it with river stones to support it.

3 Decorate the moon tree with fairy lights, totems, ribbons, symbols and baubles if you wish.

4 Empower your moon tree by lighting the fairy lights and two white nightlights at her base, repeating:
"Levanah, Queen of Heaven, I offer this sacred moon tree in your honour, and ask for your magical blessings to descend upon it."
Sit quietly and see what happens!